TENDER, TENDER

TENDER, TENDER

JESSICA JEWELL

WINNER OF THE CHARLOTTE MEW PRIZE

HEADMISTRESS PRESS

ISBN 978-1-7358236-5-2

Cover art: Marie Laurencin, detail from Music (1953) Public Domain
Cover & book design by Mary Meriam.

PUBLISHER
Headmistress Press
60 Shipview Lane
Sequim, WA 98382
Telephone: 917-428-8312
Email: headmistresspress@gmail.com
Website: headmistresspress.blogspot.com

CONTENTS

PRAYER OF ADORATION AKIN TO ASTRONOMICAL TRANSIT

At meridian, the friar plum passes between my hand and your mouth.

We use the passing to tell time in stages of ripening.

Time, we think, is measured in the pull of flesh to clingstone.

A taste? You ask, your tongue spilling out words soft as moonlight on a tranquil lake.

Ephemeral, emptiness is not filled with years, but with the desire to see one body overlap another body.

Alone we are no more than air—carbon, neon, remnants of galactic dust from the first starbirth.

We find the missing origins in the single breath our mouths share, consuming.

We saw the distant observers once but did not know the visible light was the light of our future selves.

Taste this plum from my mouth. Is it not sweet?

MILTONIOPSIS AT THE CLEVELAND BOTANICAL GARDEN

Spilling pink & imposter of pansy silk & pleasing smile,
the kind of orchid that brings blushy lemonade to bible
study & flirts over an accordion straw. The cheerleader
in some regions & in others an irritable Brontë fan.
An orchid voted most likely to marry the boy next door.
But she's also mad a lot, (or is it a deeper despair?) &
she loses it when no one's around to hear her screaming,
climbs the high woods where mule deer shed their racks,
sometimes cries, sometimes looks for a way to break
the law. She's never tried a cigarette but has slept with
a Jolly Rancher stuck in her hair. She has the most beautiful
skin, spilling pink & imposter of pansy silk & she
needs more attention than she can give right now—
somewhere warm & a good reason to bloom.

ADORATION IN THE FORM OF CALL & RESPONSE

Will you let me hold you by the wrists?
I will let you hold me by the wrists.
Will you let me kiss your ear and cheek?
I will let you kiss my lobe and gully.
Will you let my tongue explore your speech?
I will let your tongue inform translation.
Will you let my hand enshrine your sun?
I will swallow moons of your communion.
Will you give me children and a bird?
I will give you gods of seas and mountains.
Will you let my skin divine your fear?
I will cover gardens with your worship.
Will you let me take you to our bed?
I will let you hold me by the wrists.

TENDER, TENDER

Whatever she wants
is never too much

Whatever she casts
enjoins with the sea

Whatever she names
is origin lore

Whatever she ponders
the canon converts

Whatever she speaks
songbirds reprise

Whatever she mothers
is named as a god

Whatever she offers
opens a door (to)

whatever forever
for me and for more

A WALK IN WINTER IN REVERSE

The black dog eats the golden
husks of winter wheat. I ache
for her, swallow the air around
the ache the way glass aches
toward fire & takes a new form,
scalding & ochre & prone to shatter
if pulled too far. She is not too far
from here, though, I am not allowed
to solve for distance

                    O, Lord,
tell me what more you want from me
& the answer key if pushed too hard.
I light the whole air on fire, ochre &
scalding, & keep swallowing the ache
for her, the winter wheat, the black dog.

SERMON ON THE HANDS

after Aracelis Girmay

Consider the hands that write this poem.
Fingers stretched over words, molting verbs,

sluffed wings or less, feather, ink. Consider
the hands that strum the pink summit

of exclamation. My left cupping sweat
at the lip of your neck, my right, teasing cherry

from your womb.

Consider the fingers that swallow your body
from inside, as Jonah swallowed the whale whole

& lived. Give me three days & a spade & a tract
of your fertile land. Come to these hands—

one open, one knocking.

WILD GRATITUDE

If you want her again,
you should say it
with craving—
with wild and violent
gratitude, the same
as when a dry husk lips
the first rain of August.

Memory is hunger
and we are belly up
and open for the hawk.
Even the reckless
abandon us.

If you want her again,
you should learn
the edge of sharp
and shatter.
Like nature, we have
no outline.

She is sky
& I am the reed

calling the lightning down.

WHEN YOU LEAVE

Everything leaves. Everything
refuses. Everything has atmosphere.
Everything is bound for a shadow
life. Everything is its replica. Everything
replaces. Everything is tenderness.
Everything takes the air. Everything
has cellular memory. Everything long
has mountains & moons. Everything dark
has a human psyche. Everything is primordial
property. Everything forgets to breathe.
Everything is forest. Everything east
has a mouth & a sun. Everything west
is howling. Everything sleeps like snow.
Everything begins, this evening, this wanting.

INTERCESSION: STORMLIGHT

The storm arrives
again. I hear it beyond

the clouds, a lost Sandhill Crane
barking acts of moral virtues West to Sea.

The sky at first plum, then pale, a supplicant
drained of all blushing who can no longer hear

the voice of God through the wind, a lovelorn insomniac
falling asleep and not dreaming of her but in absentia,

like Methuselah dragging a stool across the horizon
looking for a place to rest or return to White Mountain
bristlecone,

a canyon of unanswered echoes, an empty spider egg dropping
from a doorframe onto the kitchen floor, the sound an iron
gate

makes shutting behind you when you leave your childhood
home for the last time and someone is waving from a darkened

window, a visitor from another lifetime you never
kissed, or a memory begging against abandonment,

that untended fire that spits, coughs,
and recedes into ash, plume ascending

like the Son to troposphere, sobbing
and fearful and full of light.

DEVOTIONAL: GHOSTS

You want our night spelled
out in the line and I want

to hear you beg
for it. I want you to savor

my words. I want you so full
and throbbing the hours flood

out of you like wet ribbons
into my mouth. I say come

over, and you do, first to bed
a then into my fingers

that have been waiting
years for your heat,

impatient as ghosts
shrieking to be seen.

PSALM IN THE KITCHEN

In the kitchen, in my kitchen, in the afternoon
light in your hair, in the black dog at the lake,
in the nibbled willow branches at Beaver Marsh,
in the god of animals, in momentum, in the oldest
of the gods, in the subtext of the translation, in
your favorite love poem, in long lines at the grocery
store again, in the brand of tissue you hoard, in
the gold stores under the earth, in the early stars,
in the stars that left us here, in the leather & gold
you leave in my bed, in some trouble with trajectory,
in the west-settling wind that moves us to kiss, in
the god of wind, in cold & warm pains, in penitence,
in the valley in the park, in the dewberry in the belly
of the blackbird, in those berries you grew your first
summer, in the missing her more than anyone you
walked away from before, in memory's missing eye
that never read you for what you needed, in the need,
in the easing of the pressures now, in cures for all
scourges, in the god of cures, in the warm light of God.

LOVE AS EXPLAINED BY QUANTUM ENTANGLEMENT

Tonight, as the light snow falls, tell yourself
that you are loved even if you are not sure.

Our moon is out there, yes, & adored, but so
is her twin who is smiling in the cold, quiet,

nova pink light of another universe. No one
has seen her, except in the timeless dark

of dreams. She tells herself that someone loves
her—a child, maybe, who once fell from her

ridges & floated away & is out there with happy
memories of her & everything is connected, honey—

can't you see it now? It's so clear, like this snow
tonight & she's out there humming a song you

once heard in a cathedral & that's when you knew
that love is tethered to all times, old & new, & that music

is a cathedral of the faithful stars & let's live now.

THE DIRECTION OF HER HUNGER

With perfect aptitude she examines her appetite
& wonders why she still resists & thus, leans
in the direction of her hunger as something winged
leans hard into a gale expecting to be cast back
into a tree or ledge. The hunger is no fledging,
has learned to hunt alone for scraps, which were first
just the illusion of nourishment but now rise in her
body like unexpected memories, throat to teeth, beg
to be chewed & thus, satisfy her. But she's not satisfied.
She's starving and looks for a woman to love her
& tame the feathers that get ruffled by gale forces.
Looks for berry-filled groves where satisfaction prowls
like something furred, a wolf, maybe, or an outcast angel,
blonde & frightened, juice clinging fast to her fangs.

CONTRITION AS LYRIC

Some will say, stop interrupting
the work of the gods. Some will
say, they know better than you
how to master your life. Some
will look at you & wonder if you
are worth petting. Some will knot
the blonde & some will whisper
devotions through cords of keratin.
Some will declare your worst art
a prophecy. Some will singe your
genius in bonfire. Some will tire
of collecting the vapor of memory.
Some will cull the heavens to find
you. Some will leave you in a
restaurant alone & some are prone
on your trophy wall. Some will fall
in love & you won't love them in return.
Some still burn you for the nicks
in their shells. Some put you through
hells & left you there smoking. Some
will crave your softest opening. Some
have hurt you & some have spoken
to the gods of war. Some want more
& more & some are still repenting.

THE FIRST DAY

I've been thinking
about how I swallow
my suffering, never
bring it
to the table, leave
it outside
for the wolves
or the moon
or an unnested
& clawed stalker
listening
for my pulse.
More passerine
than man.
More trouble
than I'm worth,
I've been told
by women
who've seen
the endless gulping.
Swallow
is a German word,
like me,
a noun, wouldn't exist
without the bird,
without her wild
& rustic,
& mud-nested,
music. Both born
afraid,
eyes closed
& naked

DEUTERONOMY 1:10 AT HOME

today you are as the stars
of heaven for multitude
& tomorrow as the stars
of earth for modesty & birds
resting in the unbranched glow
of the eveningest star
& wake to a symphonic chur
of unanswered pining
& don't you know? —God
tells us we are multitudes
in order to give us back
to our own people for tending
& isn't it wonderful? —
the humming in the meadow
lands, the star-blessed
prairies that birthed us—
yours, mine, the multitudinous
cerulean seas of our home.

EPISTOLARY PRAYER OF CONTRITION

Lord, tell me the name you gave
to the sun the day you made it.
& why does the wind eat prairies
during thunderstorms? Tell me how
many inhabitable planets there are
in the universe, & are there versions
of us somewhere else & do we ever get
a chance to meet our other selves & see
if they made the same mistakes we did,
with our time, & do we have the same names,
you & I? Or are you all things? Do you know
I once believed all the stories about you
& would cry from fear, & are you fear, too, Lord,
as well as grace? Are you the sea? Or are you
(Lord, forgive me) just a word for the sea?

INTERCESSION: THE DREAM

In each heart a similar dream:
silence's towering cathedrals,
and in each cathedral a single
answered prayer, the prayer
our memories recited upon
recognizing each other,
virtuous and paradisiacal,
or feral and tired and jagged
as a sea rock cast out from a wave.

In each wave a similar friction:
two bodies come together,
wind and water on a surface,
the disturbance that births
the hungry swell. The wave
the color of my eyes at first light.
The shore the color of yours
sliver-lit by a tidal moon.

The moony water at night
similar enough to the ink
I splash out now before you
(do you hear them, too, love,
the howl of cathedral bells?)
waiting for you to appear.

MATINS IN MEDIA RES

You tell me how God breaks
things to make them better—
Jacob, the waters, the oils,
the breads, his own son's body
on that hill of skulls & White
Acacia & even in the middle
of my suffering how he breaks
from the earth one cutting
of my life & gives back to me
a flower for grazing.

ADORATION IN THE FORM OF ADORATION

I want to dress your skin in the golden drapes
of my willful hair. I want to splice you with peach
blossoms and grow an orchard from your navel.
I want to paint crosses on your lips & swallow
communion whole. I want to atomize you, shoot
you into my veins so you can ride my heartbeat all night.
I want to trip on the tip of your tongue. I want to gulp
as recklessly as hatchlings in the cavern of your breasts.
I never want the plates under our bodies to stop moving.
I want fissure & to deify the sounds of your hailing. I want
to braid our eyelashes together with lusty tears—to sleep
between your legs as blissfully as a bee in a summer meadow.

DEUTERONOMY 13:11 IN INDIANAPOLIS

You shall eat of all clean
birds. But you shall not eat
of these: the eagle, the
vulture, & the bearded
clouds hanging over I-465
& me flying around that rainy
city dreaming about our arms
intertwined all nonchalant
in obvious aching, & the kite
by its kinds, & all ravens
by their kinds & what was the time
zone we were living in then?—
what stopped us from living
in the moment like we're doing
now, little owl & the heron after
its kind, like our kind of laughter
& easy as a late-summer smile.
You have lived in my memory
for seventeen melodies & you
may eat, sweetheart, of me
now & of all clean birds.

ABOUT THE AUTHOR

Jessica Jewell is the author of three collections of poetry, *Dust Runner, Sisi and the Girl from Town,* and *Slap Leather.* She is the co-editor of the bilingual collection, *I Hear the World Sing* and regularly publishes in both academic and literary journals. Jewell is the senior academic program director for the Wick Poetry Center at Kent State University where she also earned her MFA and PhD.

ACKNOWLEDGMENTS

Disquiet Arts:
"Adoration in the Form of Call & Response"
"Deuteronomy 1:10 At Home"
"Prayer of Adoration Akin to Astronomical Transit"

Lavender Review:
"Love in Winter as Explained by Quantum Entanglement"

Headmistress Press Books

Tender, Tender - Jessica Jewell

A Trickle of Bloom Becomes You - Jen Rouse

Cyborg Sister - Jackie Craven

Demoted Planet - Katherine Fallon

Earlier Households - Bonnie J. Morris

The Things We Bring with Us: Travel Poems - S.G. Huerta

The Water Between Us - Gillian Ebersole

Discomfort - Sarah Caulfield

The History of a Voice - Jessica Jopp

I Wish My Father - Leslèa Newman

Tender Age - Luiza Flynn-Goodlett

Low-water's Edge - Jean A. Kingsley

Routine Bloodwork - Colleen McKee

Queer Hagiographies - Audra Puchalski

Why I Never Finished My Dissertation - Laura Foley

The Princess of Pain - Carolyn Gage & Sudie Rakusin

Seed - Janice Gould

Riding with Anne Sexton - Jen Rouse

Spoiled Meat - Nicole Santalucia

Cake - Jen Rouse

The Salt and the Song - Virginia Petrucci

mad girl's crush tweet - summer jade leavitt

Saturn coming out of its Retrograde - Briana Roldan

i am this girl - gina marie bernard

Week/End - Sarah Duncan

My Girl's Green Jacket - Mary Meriam

Nuts in Nutland - Mary Meriam & Hannah Barrett

Lovely - Leslèa Newman

Teeth & Teeth - Robin Reagler

How Distant the City - Freesia McKee

Shopgirls - Marissa Higgins

Riddle - Diane Fortney

When She Woke She Was an Open Field - Hilary Brown

A Crown of Violets - Renée Vivien tr. Samantha Pious
Fireworks in the Graveyard - Joy Ladin
Social Dance - Carolyn Boll
The Force of Gratitude - Janice Gould
Spine - Sarah Caulfield
I Wore the Only Garden I've Ever Grown - Kathryn Leland
Diatribe from the Library - Farrell Greenwald Brenner
Blind Girl Grunt - Constance Merritt
Acid and Tender - Jen Rouse
Beautiful Machinery - Wendy DeGroat
Odd Mercy - Gail Thomas
The Great Scissor Hunt - Jessica K. Hylton
A Bracelet of Honeybees - Lynn Strongin
Whirlwind @ Lesbos - Risa Denenberg
The Body's Alphabet - Ann Tweedy
First name Barbie last name Doll - Maureen Bocka
Heaven to Me - Abe Louise Young
Sticky - Carter Steinmann
Tiger Laughs When You Push - Ruth Lehrer
Night Ringing - Laura Foley
Paper Cranes - Dinah Dietrich
On Loving a Saudi Girl - Carina Yun
The Burn Poems - Lynn Strongin
I Carry My Mother - Lesléa Newman
Distant Music - Joan Annsfire
The Awful Suicidal Swans - Flower Conroy
Joy Street - Laura Foley
Chiaroscuro Kisses - G.L. Morrison
The Lillian Trilogy - Mary Meriam
Lady of the Moon - Amy Lowell, Lillian Faderman, Mary Meriam
Irresistible Sonnets - ed. Mary Meriam
Lavender Review - ed. Mary Meriam

Made in the USA
Middletown, DE
19 February 2022

61302208R00022